The AI-Empowered Career: How to Use Artificial Intelligence to Boost Your Career

Written By Richard Aragon

I0406957

Introduction

When I was a teenager, my girlfriend at the time had a father that worked in the printing industry. All throughout her childhood and through most of her life, her father held a good paying and respectable job. By this time though, printing presses were an ancient relic. I watched his career prospects dry up completely, in only a matter of years. In the age of digitization, his skills were no longer necessary.

I remember watching this man in his early 50's try in every way he could to reinvent a new career for himself. He ended up taking the most menial jobs he could find, because he had no other professional skills in any other area. I remember watching that and thinking to myself that I will plan every aspect of my life if I have to, in order to make sure that never happens to me.

So, that is exactly what I did. Early on in my career, I had a choice between a marketing career and an IT career. Marketing paid more upfront, and was more glamorous. IT paid more in the long term and seemed like the surest long term on the planet at the time, so I went all in on IT.

From the moment I first laid eyes on AI, I knew there was going to be a groundswell of change, and that it would directly impact me and my career. The past six months have been like nothing I have ever seen before in the IT industry. Huge, coordinated layoffs, hiring freezes, salary reductions. The industry is going through a

1

significant shift. It will not be the same industry in 5 years as it is today.

From the very first moment I began thinking these thoughts, I thought of the man in the story I wrote out above. As a member of the last generation born into an analog world, with my early childhood being completely analog, I have seen these changes before. When such change occurs, you can either embrace it, or be left behind. Complaining about it or wishing it would not change does nothing to help your future in the face of those choices. This book is written for anyone who may be facing that same choice.

Chapter 1: Introduction to AI

Artificial intelligence (AI) is one of the most transformative technologies of our time. At its core, AI refers to computer systems or machines that are capable of performing tasks that typically require human intelligence and cognition.

To understand AI, it helps to first define intelligence. Intelligence can be thought of as the ability to acquire knowledge and skills and apply them to solve problems. Human intelligence involves abilities like learning, reasoning, problem-solving, perception, creativity and adaptation. The overarching goal of AI is to replicate these types of capabilities in computer systems.

The concept of AI dates back to the 1950s when scientists and researchers began exploring the possibility of machines that could think and act like humans. In the decades since, AI has gone through periods of optimism and hype as well as setbacks.

However, in recent years AI has seen major advancements due to a convergence of key factors:

Increased computational power and the ability to process huge datasets

The availability of large amounts of data to train AI algorithms on

Progress in machine learning methods such as deep learning neural networks

Significant improvements in AI hardware including graphics processing units (GPUs)

Today, AI has become ubiquitous in many products and services we use. For example:

Virtual assistants like Siri, Alexa and Google Assistant use natural language processing to understand human speech and respond. Social media platforms utilize AI to recognize faces and objects in photos and videos.

Autonomous vehicles integrate computer vision, sensors and machine learning to navigate without human input.

Healthcare organizations are applying AI techniques like pattern recognition to medical images to assist in diagnosing diseases.

Looking ahead, AI is poised to transform major sectors like transportation, healthcare, finance and manufacturing. It raises important questions around the future of work, privacy, bias and social impacts. Careful oversight and governance will be needed to develop AI responsibly and ethically.

In summary, artificial intelligence refers broadly to machines that are capable of human-like cognition such as learning, perceiving, reasoning and problem solving. After decades of research and development, AI applications are now widespread in daily life. As the technology continues to advance, AI aims to provide new capabilities that will augment human intelligence for the betterment of society.

How is AI Changing the World of Work?

Artificial intelligence is having a major impact on the workplace and transforming how work gets done. Here are some of the key ways AI is changing the nature of work:

Automating Tasks and Workflows: AI is automating routine, repetitive tasks in many jobs - from processing paperwork to cleaning data. This allows human workers to focus on higher-value work. AI tools can also automate complex workflows end-to-end.

Augmenting Human Capabilities: AI is augmenting human skills rather than replacing jobs entirely. For example, AI can help salespeople analyze customer data to make better recommendations or help doctors interpret medical images more accurately.

Creating New Kinds of Jobs: While AI is automating some jobs, it is also creating new kinds of jobs - like AI trainers, explainability experts, data labelers, and chatbot designers. New roles are emerging that support AI workflows.

Improving Decision Making: AI can digest huge amounts of structured and unstructured data to detect patterns. This enables more informed business decision making across areas like risk analysis, process optimization, and predictive analytics.

Enhancing Customer Service: Intelligent AI chatbots and virtual agents can provide personalized customer service at scale 24/7. This improves customer satisfaction.

Increasing Business Efficiency: AI streamlines and optimize business processes to drive greater productivity, efficiency and growth. It can provide cost savings and competitive advantages.

The impact of AI on work will continue to accelerate. While some jobs may be at risk, AI is creating opportunities for developing new skills, taking on more strategic roles and innovating new businesses. With the right strategies, AI can augment human capabilities and create valuable synergies.

Why is it Important to Upskill for the Age of AI?

As AI becomes more integrated into every industry and function, it's crucial that professionals take time to upskill themselves to remain competitive in the age of artificial intelligence. Here are some key reasons upskilling is important:

Reduce Risk of Job Displacement: Tasks that are repetitive and routine tend to be the most susceptible to automation with AI. Upskilling helps create a future-proof skillset and prepares workers for taking on more cognitive, creative responsibilities that are less likely to be displaced.

Become an AI Expert: There is a huge demand for roles like AI researchers, data scientists, machine learning engineers to develop, apply and manage AI systems. Upskilling allows tapping into these in-demand jobs.

Apply AI to Current Roles: Nearly every job today can be augmented with AI capabilities in some way. For example, marketers can upskill to use AI for personalized ad targeting, predictive analytics and automated content creation. Upskilling makes workers adept at applying AI purposefully.

Complement AI Capabilities: AI can enhance but not replicate more complex human skills like creativity, empathy, leadership, communication and strategy. Upskilling helps sharpen these complementary capabilities.

Gain a Competitive Edge: Increasing one's tech skills and AI literacy provides professionals with a distinct competitive advantage. Even basic AI upskilling can help gain an edge.

Prepare for Team Collaboration: As companies adopt AI solutions, they require teams with both technical and non-technical members to work synergistically. Upskilling enables effective collaboration with AI systems.

Continuous learning and upskilling in domains like data science, machine learning, and human-AI interaction are key to professional success in our AI future. Investing time to upskill will ensure individuals remain uniquely valuable, multi-dimensional contributors.

Chapter 2: Identifying Your AI-Transferable Skills

What are AI-Transferable Skills?
As artificial intelligence becomes more prevalent, professionals need to identify and develop the human skills that will remain uniquely valuable alongside AI capabilities. These "AI-transferable" skills allow human workers to augment their expertise using AI rather than be replaced. Some of the most important AI-transferable skills include:
Critical Thinking - With AI systems making recommendations or generating content, humans need the discernment to ask good questions and determine if the outputs make sense. For example, a marketer could utilize an AI content creation tool, but needs critical thinking to edit and refine the draft for relevance. Developing the capacity for judgment, strategic reasoning and assessing alternatives will be key.
Creativity - AI excels at optimizing existing processes but creative thinking is still a profoundly human skill. Creativity will be essential for finding innovative ways to integrate AI tools into business operations to drive efficiencies and new value. For example, a customer service representative could use AI to analyze customer data and identifiable trends, but still needs human creativity to develop empathetic solutions.
Cross-domain Adaptability - As companies transform functions through AI adoption, professionals will need the self-awareness and motivation to continuously learn new skills and adapt to changing roles. Having flexibility and a growth mindset will enable workers to remain agile. A willingness to expand beyond one's comfort zone and expertise will be essential.
Data Literacy - Basic data skills like data collection, evaluation, analysis, visualization and storytelling will allow professionals to be proactive stakeholders in deploying AI tools. Rather than passively

receiving AI outcomes, data literacy empowers professionals to focus AI on business priorities. For example, HR managers could utilize data skills to synthesize employee retention factors, rather than just implement an off-the-shelf predictive attrition model. Emotional Intelligence - AI currently lacks human qualities like empathy. Skills like cooperation, communication, reading emotions and influencing will continue to set humans apart. Workers can combine their emotional intelligence with AI capabilities to make processes more intuitive and human-centric. For example, an AI chatbot integrated with emotional intelligence can pick up on frustrated customers and seamlessly transfer them to a human agent.

In total, developing a diverse range of technical and soft skills will prepare professionals to actively shape the role of AI in business - not just passively receive it. The most adaptable professionals will meet AI capabilities with their own complementary human strengths.

How to Identify Your AI-Transferable Skills

With artificial intelligence growing more capable, it's important for professionals to take stock of their skills that will remain uniquely human. Conducting an AI-transferable skills assessment allows you to proactively prepare for working alongside AI. Here are steps to identify your most relevant capabilities:

Review your soft skills - Make a list of the social and emotional skills you possess, like communication, persuasion, collaboration, empathy, adaptability, etc. These qualities are intrinsically human and difficult for AI to replicate. Soft skills help build trust in AI systems.

Analyze your hard skills - Identify more technical skills like critical thinking, problem-solving, research, data analysis, writing, design etc. Consider how these skills allow you to complement AI capabilities in your current role. For example, design skills help a marketer integrate AI product recommendation engines.

Map your creative process - Outline your approach to open-ended tasks like developing a new strategy or designing a creative project. The nonlinear, complex nature of human creativity is hard for AI to match and automate.

Understand how AI could augment your work - Make a list of responsibilities in your job that AI could potentially automate. Then identify areas where AI would actually provide augmentation and support rather than replacing you. This reveals opportunities to apply your complementary human skills.

Identify skill gaps - Determine areas such as data literacy, computational thinking, design, etc. where upskilling could help you collaborate with AI more seamlessly. Commit to filling these gaps by pursuing online courses, certifications, or training.

Talk to leaders in your field - Have candid discussions with managers and mentors about the skills they foresee remaining resilient in your industry as AI adoption accelerates. Incorporate their insights into your skill assessment.

Conducting an honest inventory of your AI-transferable skills empowers you to be proactive about your career. Rather than compete, developing technical and soft skills enables you to collaborate with AI and focus on the responsibilities that fully leverage your innate human strengths. This assessment provides clarity for upskilling.

How to Develop Your AI-Transferable Skills

In a rapidly evolving job market where artificial intelligence is becoming increasingly integrated into various industries, it's essential to develop AI-transferable skills that can help you stay relevant and advance in your career. These skills not only make you a valuable asset to your current employer but also open up new opportunities for growth and innovation. In this chapter, we will explore practical steps to help you cultivate these skills effectively.

1. Understand the Basics of AI

Before you can begin developing AI-transferable skills, it's crucial to have a fundamental understanding of what AI is and how it works. You don't need to become an AI expert, but grasping the basic concepts is essential. Start by reading introductory materials, taking online courses, or attending workshops that provide an overview of artificial intelligence, machine learning, and deep learning.

2. Learn Data Analysis and Data Science

One of the cornerstones of AI is data. To work effectively with AI, you must be proficient in data analysis and data science. This includes understanding data collection, cleaning, and preprocessing, as well as statistical analysis and visualization. You can find numerous online courses and resources that teach data science skills using programming languages like Python and R.

3. Master Machine Learning

Machine learning is the driving force behind many AI applications. Learning how to create and deploy machine learning models is a valuable skill. Start with online courses and tutorials on platforms like Coursera, edX, or Udacity. Experiment with open-source machine learning libraries like TensorFlow and scikit-learn to gain practical experience.

4. Develop Programming Skills

Programming is the backbone of AI development. Familiarize yourself with programming languages commonly used in AI, such as Python and R. These languages are versatile and have extensive libraries and frameworks for AI development. Practice coding and work on AI-related projects to build your programming proficiency.

5. Embrace Cloud Computing

Many AI projects require significant computational resources. Cloud computing platforms like Amazon Web Services (AWS), Microsoft Azure, and Google Cloud provide access to powerful AI tools and resources. Learn how to use these platforms for data storage, processing, and AI model training.

6. Hone Your Problem-Solving Skills

AI is all about solving complex problems. Practice critical thinking and problem-solving by tackling AI-related challenges, participating in data science competitions (such as Kaggle), or working on real-world AI projects. Collaborating with others in the AI community can also help you develop these skills.

7. Stay Informed and Adapt

The field of AI is constantly evolving. To remain competitive in your career, stay informed about the latest AI trends, research, and technologies. Follow AI-related news, join AI-focused online communities, and attend conferences or webinars. Adaptability is key to thriving in the AI-powered job market.

8. Seek Professional Development Opportunities

Many organizations offer training and development programs related to AI. Take advantage of these opportunities to enhance your AI-transferable skills. If your employer doesn't provide such programs, consider pursuing relevant certifications or advanced degrees in AI or related fields.

9. Build a Portfolio

Create a portfolio showcasing your AI-related projects and accomplishments. A strong portfolio demonstrates your skills and can be a valuable asset when seeking new career opportunities or promotions.

10. Network and Collaborate

Connect with professionals in the AI field, both inside and outside your organization. Networking can lead to valuable collaborations, mentorship opportunities, and access to AI projects that allow you to apply and further develop your skills.

By following these steps and continuously investing in your AI-transferable skills, you can position yourself as a valuable asset in the AI-driven job market. Whether you're in marketing, healthcare, finance, or any other industry, these skills will empower you to harness the potential of artificial intelligence and boost your career to new heights.

Chapter 3: Exploring AI Career Opportunities

Different types of AI careers
Artificial intelligence (AI) is a rapidly growing field with a wide range of career opportunities. AI professionals are needed in a variety of industries, including technology, healthcare, finance, and manufacturing.
Here are some of the most popular types of AI careers:
Machine learning engineer: Machine learning engineers develop and deploy machine learning models. They work with large datasets to train models to make predictions or decisions.
Data scientist: Data scientists collect, clean, and analyze data to extract insights. They use their skills to develop data-driven solutions to business problems.
Software engineer: Software engineers design, develop, and test software applications. They use their skills to build AI-powered applications that can automate tasks, make predictions, and interact with users.
Research scientist: Research scientists conduct research on new AI technologies and algorithms. They work to develop new and innovative ways to use AI to solve real-world problems.
Robotics engineer: Robotics engineers design, build, and test robots. They use their skills to develop AI-powered robots that can perform complex tasks in a variety of environments.
Natural language processing (NLP) engineer: NLP engineers develop and deploy NLP models. They work with language data to train models to understand and generate human language.
Computer vision engineer: Computer vision engineers develop and deploy computer vision models. They work with image and video data to train models to recognize and identify objects and scenes.

AI product manager: AI product managers develop and launch AI-powered products. They work with engineers, designers, and marketers to bring AI products to market.

AI business analyst: AI business analysts help businesses understand and implement AI solutions. They work with stakeholders to identify business problems that can be solved with AI and to develop and implement AI solutions.

AI ethicist: AI ethicists work to ensure that AI is developed and used in an ethical and responsible manner. They work with engineers, policymakers, and other stakeholders to develop and implement AI ethics guidelines.

These are just a few of the many types of AI careers available. As the field of AI continues to grow, new and innovative AI careers will continue to emerge.

If you are interested in a career in AI, there are a few things you can do to prepare. First, it is important to have a strong foundation in mathematics, statistics, and computer science. You should also learn about different AI technologies and algorithms. Additionally, it is important to develop your problem-solving and analytical skills.

There are a number of resources available to help you prepare for a career in AI. You can find online courses and tutorials on AI topics. You can also attend bootcamps and certification programs. Additionally, many universities offer AI degree programs.

With the right skills and training, you can launch a successful and rewarding career in AI.

How to Find AI Jobs

Artificial intelligence presents exciting career opportunities for professionals across industries and skill sets. Here are some proactive tips to find open roles that leverage your AI skills:

Broaden your search terms - Look for position titles like "Machine Learning Engineer," "AI Solutions Architect," "Robotic Process Automation Developer," "Computer Vision Engineer," "AI Ethicist," and related roles. Widen your scope beyond just "Data Scientist."

Leverage LinkedIn - Follow companies actively using AI like tech giants, research labs, and startups. Search for AI-related titles within those companies and set job alerts. Join relevant LinkedIn groups to uncover openings.

Check company career pages - Look directly at the careers section of major technology companies leading in AI like Google, Microsoft, Meta, NVIDIA, and IBM. Browse any AI research divisions.

Attend industry events - Conferences and seminars on AI application areas like self-driving cars, fintech, and robotics help build connections and uncover unlisted opportunities.

Gain practical experience - Complete online courses, certifications, or clubs related to AI skills like deep learning and natural language processing to gain hands-on skills and build out your resume/portfolio.

Consider internships - Entry-level internships at AI labs, startups or R&D divisions provide valuable real-world experience to kickstart your career. Keep an open mind.

Talk to your network - Connect with professors, colleagues, friends employed in the AI field to get insider perspective and ask for any open referrals.

Check non-tech companies - All industries from healthcare to agriculture are adopting AI. Don't overlook AI openings in less traditional sectors.

Follow leaders in AI - Track thought leaders, innovators, and professionals in the AI field via blogs, social media, publications to find exciting companies and roles.

Set Google Alerts - Get automated notifications of new AI job listings by establishing alerts for relevant keywords like "AI internship" and "conversational AI."

With some focus and creativity, there are many paths to find rewarding roles applying AI for impact. Continuously expanding your skillset and network improves your odds of landing your ideal job.

How to Prepare for AI Job Interviews

Landing a job in the field of artificial intelligence (AI) can be both exciting and challenging. AI job interviews often require a combination of technical expertise, problem-solving skills, and a deep understanding of AI concepts. To help you excel in your AI job interviews, this chapter provides a comprehensive guide on how to prepare effectively.

1. Understand the Job Requirements

Before diving into your interview preparation, it's crucial to have a clear understanding of the specific job role and its requirements. AI is a broad field, encompassing machine learning, natural language processing, computer vision, and more. Tailor your preparation to match the job description and its technical demands.

2. Review Core AI Concepts

Expect questions about fundamental AI concepts in your interviews. Make sure you are well-versed in topics such as supervised learning, unsupervised learning, reinforcement learning, neural networks, and deep learning. Revisit your AI textbooks or take online courses if needed to refresh your knowledge.

3. Brush Up on Algorithms and Data Structures

A strong grasp of algorithms and data structures is essential for AI positions. Review commonly used algorithms and data structures like sorting, searching, graphs, and trees. Be prepared to apply these concepts to AI-related problems.

4. Coding and Technical Assessments

Many AI interviews include coding or technical assessments. Practice coding challenges related to AI, data analysis, and machine learning on platforms like LeetCode, HackerRank, or Kaggle. These platforms often have specific AI-related sections to help you prepare.

5. Machine Learning and Deep Learning

If the job involves machine learning or deep learning, be ready to discuss various algorithms and their applications. Understand how to preprocess data, create and train models, and evaluate their performance. Be prepared to explain your choices in model selection and hyperparameter tuning.

6. Data Science Skills

For roles involving data science, review data manipulation techniques, feature engineering, and data visualization. Familiarize yourself with data science libraries like pandas, scikit-learn, and Matplotlib in Python.

7. Real-World Projects

Highlight any real-world AI projects you've worked on. Discuss your role, the challenges you faced, and the results you achieved. Be ready to provide examples of how you've applied AI to solve practical problems.

8. Behavioral Questions

In addition to technical questions, expect behavioral questions that assess your teamwork, problem-solving abilities, and adaptability. Use the STAR (Situation, Task, Action, Result) method to structure your responses.

9. Stay Informed About AI Trends

Keep up with the latest developments in AI by reading research papers, following AI news, and engaging with AI communities online. This knowledge can help you discuss current AI trends and demonstrate your passion for the field.

10. Mock Interviews

Conduct mock interviews with friends, mentors, or online platforms that offer interview practice. This will help you get comfortable with the interview format and receive constructive feedback.

11. Ask Questions

Prepare thoughtful questions to ask your interviewers. This demonstrates your interest in the role and the company. Questions about the team's projects, AI tools and technologies used, and the company's AI strategy can be insightful.

12. Professional Presence

Dress professionally and arrive on time for in-person interviews. In virtual interviews, ensure your video and audio setup is reliable. Maintain good eye contact, speak clearly, and listen actively during the interview.

13. Follow Up

After the interview, send a thank-you email expressing your appreciation for the opportunity and reiterating your interest in the position. This small gesture can leave a positive impression.

Remember that AI job interviews are as much about demonstrating your problem-solving abilities and practical skills as they are about showcasing your passion for AI. By thoroughly preparing and presenting yourself as a knowledgeable and enthusiastic candidate, you'll be well on your way to a successful AI career. Good luck!

Chapter 4: Using AI to Enhance Your Current Job

How to use AI to automate tasks

AI can be used to automate a wide range of tasks, from simple to complex. Here are some examples of how you can use AI to automate tasks in your work:

Use AI to automate data entry. AI can be used to extract data from documents and images, and to populate databases and spreadsheets. This can free up your time so that you can focus on more important tasks.

Use AI to automate customer service tasks. AI can be used to chat with customers, answer questions, and resolve issues. This can help you to improve customer satisfaction and reduce costs.

Use AI to automate marketing tasks. AI can be used to generate personalized marketing campaigns, target the right audience, and measure the results of your campaigns. This can help you to improve your marketing ROI.

Use AI to automate sales tasks. AI can be used to qualify leads, generate personalized sales pitches, and close deals. This can help you to increase your sales.

Use AI to automate product development tasks. AI can be used to analyze customer data, identify trends, and develop new products. This can help you to bring new products to market faster and meet the needs of your customers.

To automate a task with AI, you can use a variety of different tools and services. Some popular AI automation tools include:

Zapier: Zapier is a workflow automation tool that allows you to connect different apps and services together. You can use Zapier to create automated workflows that trigger actions when certain events occur. For example, you could create a Zap that sends you an email notification when a new lead is generated in your CRM system.

Microsoft Power Automate: Microsoft Power Automate is another popular workflow automation tool. It is similar to Zapier, but it is specifically designed for Microsoft products and services.

Google Cloud Platform AI Platform: Google Cloud Platform AI Platform is a suite of AI tools and services that allows you to develop, train, and deploy AI models. You can use AI Platform to automate tasks such as image recognition, natural language processing, and machine learning.

In addition to these general-purpose AI automation tools, there are also a number of specialized AI automation tools available for specific industries and tasks. For example, there are AI automation tools for customer service, sales, marketing, and product development.

To choose the right AI automation tool for your needs, consider the following factors:

The types of tasks you want to automate

The budget you have available

The level of technical expertise required

The level of integration you need with other systems

Once you have chosen an AI automation tool, you can start creating automated workflows. To do this, you will need to identify the steps involved in the task you want to automate and then create a workflow that triggers the appropriate actions at each step.

For example, if you want to automate the process of sending a welcome email to new customers, you would create a workflow that triggers an email notification when a new customer is created in your CRM system. The workflow would then send the welcome email to the new customer.

AI automation can be a great way to save time and improve efficiency in your work. By automating repetitive tasks, you can free up your time so that you can focus on more important things.

Here are some additional tips for using AI to automate tasks:

Start by automating small, simple tasks. This will help you to learn the basics of AI automation and to see how it can benefit your work. Once you have mastered automating simple tasks, you can start to automate more complex tasks.

Don't be afraid to experiment. There are many different ways to automate tasks with AI. Try different approaches and see what works best for you.

Monitor your automated workflows regularly. Make sure that they are working as expected and that they are not causing any problems.

AI automation is a powerful tool that can help you to improve your productivity and efficiency. By following the tips above, you can start using AI to automate tasks in your work today.

How to Use AI to Make Better Decisions

AI systems can analyze massive amounts of data to uncover patterns and insights that can inform improved decision making. Here are some best practices:

Determine decision requirements - Define the type of decision being made, key objectives, and success metrics to guide the AI.

Curate reliable data - Ensure quality data that is comprehensive, unbiased and relevant to the decision context.

Select appropriate AI model - Match the AI algorithm to the problem. Options include rules-based systems, machine learning, neural networks, etc.

Start with hybrid approach - Build trust by having AI generate recommendations, while still having humans make the final call.

Continuously re-train - Feed decisions back into the AI to further train it on new data and edge cases.

Explainability is key - Require AI providers to offer model explanations to understand drivers behind recommendations.

Test extensively - Validate models by having AI and human experts weigh in and compare decisions. Refine until aligned.

Monitor for fairness - Proactively audit for biases and unacceptable errors to avoid harmful AI decisions.

Keep humans in the loop - Have experienced professionals monitor and override AI if questionable recommendations arise.

With the right approach, AI can complement human judgment and improve the speed and accuracy of decision making. However, human oversight remains essential.

How to Use AI to Collaborate with Others

AI systems like intelligent assistants and chatbots are making it easier for teams to collaborate. Here are some tips:

Use AI for research - Have AI summarize reports, analyze data, find relevant information to feed into group discussions.

Automate repetitive tasks - Free up teams from mundane work and let AI handle tasks like scheduling meetings, compiling status reports, updating spreadsheets.

Facilitate brainstorming - Use AI ideation tools to provide fresh prompts and perspectives when collaborating on new ideas.

Increase accessibility - Enable voice-driven interfaces so collaborators can interact hands-free with AI systems. Helpful for differently abled teammates.

Support remote teams - Intelligent chatbots allow seamless connection across locations. AI can transcribe meetings and indexed key discussion points.

Multitask during meetings - Use voice assistants to compile notes, retrieve relevant documents, add action items while collaborating in person.

Automate status updates - Chatbots can provide quick project status reports to collaborators when out of office.

Translate conversations - In global teams, use AI real-time translation to remove language barriers during meetings and discussions.

Analyze team dynamics - Collect and process collaboration data with AI to provide insights on improving team effectiveness.

With some creativity, AI can make collaborating on complex tasks more productive and inclusive. It streamlines coordination while keeping human teamwork at the center.

Chapter 5: Upskilling Using Generative AI

What is generative AI?

Generative AI is a type of artificial intelligence that can create new content, such as text, code, images, and music. It does this by learning from large datasets of existing content and then using that knowledge to generate new content that is similar in style and quality.

Generative AI is still a relatively new technology, but it is rapidly developing and has the potential to revolutionize many industries and professions. It is already being used to create new products and services, automate tasks, and help people to be more creative.

How is generative AI changing the world of work?

Generative AI is changing the world of work in a number of ways. First, it is automating many tasks that were previously done by humans. For example, generative AI is now being used to write articles, generate marketing copy, and design products. This is freeing up workers to focus on more creative and strategic tasks.

Second, generative AI is creating new opportunities for workers. For example, generative AI is being used to develop new products and services, such as AI-powered virtual assistants and AI-generated creative content. This is creating new jobs and industries.

Finally, generative AI is helping workers to be more productive and efficient. For example, generative AI can be used to automate tasks, generate insights from data, and collaborate with others. This is helping workers to get more done in less time.

Why should you use generative AI to upskill your career?

Generative AI is a powerful tool that can help you to upskill your career in a number of ways. First, it can help you to learn new skills. For example, you can use generative AI to learn how to code, write, design, or create music.

Second, generative AI can help you to create content. For example, you can use generative AI to write articles, generate marketing copy, or design products. This can help you to save time and produce high-quality content.

Third, generative AI can help you to automate tasks. For example, you can use generative AI to automate tasks such as data entry, customer service, and social media marketing. This can free up your time so that you can focus on more important tasks.

Finally, generative AI can help you to collaborate with others. For example, you can use generative AI to share ideas, brainstorm solutions, and create joint projects. This can help you to be more productive and efficient.

Overall, generative AI is a powerful tool that can help you to upskill your career in a number of ways. By learning how to use generative AI, you can make yourself more valuable to employers and increase your chances of success in the future of work.

Types of generative AI

Generative AI can be divided into five main categories: text-based, code-based, image-based, audio-based, and video-based.

Text-based generative AI

Text-based generative AI models can generate new text, such as articles, blog posts, and even books. They are trained on large datasets of existing text, and they learn to identify patterns in the data. This allows them to generate new text that is similar in style and quality to the text they were trained on.

Some popular examples of text-based generative AI models include:

GPT-3: GPT-3 is a large language model from OpenAI that can generate text, translate languages, write different kinds of creative content, and answer your questions in an informative way.

LaMDA: LaMDA is a large language model from Google AI that can generate different creative text formats of text content, like poems, code, scripts, musical pieces, email, letters, etc.

Megatron-Turing NLG: Megatron-Turing NLG is a large language model from NVIDIA that can generate different creative text formats of text content, like poems, code, scripts, musical pieces, email, letters, etc.

Code-based generative AI

Code-based generative AI models can generate new code, such as functions, classes, and modules. They are trained on large datasets of existing code, and they learn to identify patterns in the data. This allows them to generate new code that is similar in style and functionality to the code they were trained on.

Some popular examples of code-based generative AI models include:

GitHub Copilot: GitHub Copilot is a code-generation tool that suggests code completions and functions as you type. It is trained on a massive dataset of public GitHub code.

CodeGen: CodeGen is a code-generation tool that can generate code in a variety of programming languages. It is trained on a massive dataset of public code.

TabNine: TabNine is a code-generation tool that can generate code completions and functions as you type. It is trained on a massive dataset of public and private code.

Image-based generative AI

Image-based generative AI models can generate new images, such as photos, paintings, and illustrations. They are trained on large datasets of existing images, and they learn to identify patterns in the data. This allows them to generate new images that are similar in style and quality to the images they were trained on.

Some popular examples of image-based generative AI models include:

DALL-E 2: DALL-E 2 is an image-generation model from OpenAI that can generate images from text descriptions.

Imagen: Imagen is an image-generation model from Google AI that can generate images from text descriptions.

Parti: Parti is an image-generation model from NVIDIA that can generate images from text descriptions.

Audio-based generative AI

Audio-based generative AI models can generate new audio, such as music, speech, and sound effects. They are trained on large datasets of existing audio, and they learn to identify patterns in the data. This allows them to generate new audio that is similar in style and quality to the audio they were trained on.

Some popular examples of audio-based generative AI models include:

MuseNet: MuseNet is a music-generation model from Google AI that can generate music in a variety of styles.

Jukebox: Jukebox is a music-generation model from OpenAI that can generate music in a variety of styles.

AudioLM: AudioLM is a speech-generation model from Google AI that can generate speech in a variety of voices and styles.

Video-based generative AI

Video-based generative AI models can generate new videos, such as movies, TV shows, and video games. They are trained on large datasets of existing videos, and they learn to identify patterns in the data. This allows them to generate new videos that are similar in style and quality to the videos they were trained on.

Some popular examples of video-based generative AI models include:

Imagen Video: Imagen Video is a video-generation model from Google AI that can generate videos from text descriptions.
Parti Video: Parti Video is a video-generation model from NVIDIA that can generate videos from text descriptions.
Meta AI Video: Meta AI Video is a video-generation model from Meta AI that can generate videos from text descriptions.
These are just a few examples of the many types of generative AI models that are available. As generative AI continues to develop, new and innovative models are emerging all the time.

How to use generative AI to upskill your career
Generative AI can be used to upskill your career in a number of ways. Here are a few examples:
Use generative AI to learn new skills
Generative AI can be used to learn new skills in a variety of ways. For example, you can use generative AI to:
Learn a new programming language
Learn how to write different kinds of creative content
Learn how to design websites or apps
Learn how to play a musical instrument
To learn a new skill using generative AI, you can use a variety of tools and resources. For example, you can use a code-generation tool to learn how to code. You can use a text-generation tool to learn how to write different kinds of creative content. You can use an image-generation tool to learn how to design websites or apps. And you can use an audio-generation tool to learn how to play a musical instrument.
Use generative AI to create content
Generative AI can be used to create a variety of content, such as:
Articles
Blog posts
Books
Marketing copy
Product descriptions
Social media posts
To create content using generative AI, you can use a variety of tools and resources. For example, you can use a text-generation tool to write articles, blog posts, and books. You can use an image-generation tool to create product descriptions and social media posts. And you can use an audio-generation tool to create podcasts and videos.
Use generative AI to automate tasks

Generative AI can be used to automate a variety of tasks, such as:
Data entry
Customer service
Social media marketing
Product development
Research
To automate tasks using generative AI, you can use a variety of tools and resources. For example, you can use a text-generation tool to automate customer service tasks. You can use an image-generation tool to automate product development tasks. And you can use an audio-generation tool to automate research tasks.
Use generative AI to collaborate with others
Generative AI can be used to collaborate with others in a variety of ways. For example, you can use generative AI to:
Brainstorm ideas
Generate solutions to problems
Create joint projects
To collaborate with others using generative AI, you can use a variety of tools and resources. For example, you can use a text-generation tool to brainstorm ideas with others. You can use an image-generation tool to generate solutions to problems with others. And you can use an audio-generation tool to create joint projects with others.
Generative AI is a powerful tool that can help you to upskill your career in a number of ways. By following the tips above, you can start using generative AI to learn new skills, create content, automate tasks, and collaborate with others.

Examples of generative AI in use
Here are a few examples of generative AI in use today:
GitHub Copilot: GitHub Copilot is a code-generation tool that suggests code completions and functions as you type. It is trained on a massive dataset of public GitHub code. GitHub Copilot can be used to automate many tasks, such as writing repetitive code, generating documentation, and refactoring code. This can help programmers to be more productive and efficient.
DALL-E 2: DALL-E 2 is an image-generation model from OpenAI that can generate images from text descriptions. DALL-E 2 can be used to create images for a variety of purposes, such as product design, advertising, and entertainment. For example, DALL-E 2 can be used to generate a new product design from a text description,

create an advertising image for a new product, or generate a scene from a movie or TV show.

Jasper AI: Jasper AI is a text-generation tool that can generate a variety of content, such as articles, blog posts, marketing copy, and product descriptions. Jasper AI can be used to automate many tasks, such as writing content for websites and blogs, creating marketing campaigns, and generating product descriptions. This can help writers and marketers to be more productive and efficient.

Runway ML: Runway ML is a platform that provides access to a variety of generative AI tools. Runway ML can be used to generate text, code, images, audio, and video. Runway ML can be used for a variety of purposes, such as product design, advertising, and entertainment. For example, Runway ML can be used to generate a new product design from a text description, create an advertising image for a new product, or generate a scene from a movie or TV show.

These are just a few examples of the many ways that generative AI is being used today. As generative AI continues to develop, we can expect to see even more innovative and groundbreaking applications in the future.

Here are some additional examples of generative AI in use:

In the healthcare industry, generative AI is being used to develop new drugs and treatments, diagnose diseases, and personalize patient care. For example, generative AI is being used to develop new drugs that are more effective and have fewer side effects. It is also being used to diagnose diseases more accurately and to personalize patient care based on individual needs.

In the financial industry, generative AI is being used to detect fraud, predict market trends, and develop new financial products. For example, generative AI is being used to detect fraudulent transactions and to predict stock prices. It is also being used to develop new financial products, such as personalized investment plans and insurance policies.

In the manufacturing industry, generative AI is being used to design new products, optimize production lines, and improve quality control. For example, generative AI is being used to design new products that are more efficient and durable. It is also being used to optimize production lines to reduce waste and improve efficiency. Additionally, generative AI is being used to improve quality control by identifying defects in products.

Generative AI is a powerful tool that has the potential to revolutionize many industries and professions. As generative AI continues to develop, we can expect to see even more innovative and groundbreaking applications in the future.

Tips for Using Generative AI to Upskill Your Career

Generative AI, a subset of artificial intelligence, is revolutionizing the way we create content, make decisions, and solve complex problems. It's a powerful tool that can significantly enhance your career when used effectively. In this chapter, we'll explore practical tips for leveraging generative AI to upskill yourself and stay ahead in your professional journey.

1. Understand Generative AI Basics

Before diving into the practical applications, take some time to understand the fundamentals of generative AI. Familiarize yourself with the concepts of neural networks, natural language processing (NLP), and generative models like GPT (Generative Pre-trained Transformer). This foundational knowledge will help you use generative AI more effectively.

2. Identify Relevance to Your Field

Generative AI can be applied in various industries and domains, from content generation to data analysis. Identify how generative AI is relevant to your specific field or career goals. This could involve automating repetitive tasks, enhancing creativity, or improving decision-making.

3. Explore AI-Powered Content Creation

Generative AI can assist in creating written content, visuals, and even music. If your career involves content creation, consider using AI tools to generate drafts, brainstorm ideas, or design graphics. For example, AI-driven text generators can help with blog posts, reports, and marketing materials.

4. Enhance Decision-Making with AI Insights

Generative AI can analyze large datasets and provide valuable insights. If you work in a data-driven profession, leverage AI-powered analytics tools to uncover trends, make predictions, and optimize strategies. This can be particularly valuable in fields like finance, marketing, and healthcare.

5. Automate Routine Tasks

AI can handle repetitive and time-consuming tasks, freeing up your time for more strategic work. Identify tasks in your daily routine that could be automated with generative AI. This might include data entry, scheduling, or customer support.

6. Personalize Learning and Development

Generative AI can help create personalized learning materials. Use AI-driven recommendation systems to find relevant courses, articles, and resources to upskill in your career. AI can also assist in generating personalized learning content tailored to your specific needs.

7. Collaborate with AI-Enhanced Tools

AI can be a valuable collaborator. In fields like research, you can work alongside AI algorithms to analyze data, explore hypotheses, and generate insights. This collaborative approach can lead to more efficient and innovative outcomes.

8. Stay Ethical and Responsible

As you incorporate generative AI into your career, be mindful of ethical considerations. Understand bias in AI models, data privacy, and responsible AI usage. Ensure that the AI solutions you adopt align with ethical standards and industry regulations.

9. Keep Learning and Experimenting

Generative AI technologies evolve rapidly. Stay up to date with the latest developments by following AI research, attending workshops, and experimenting with new tools. Continual learning and experimentation are essential for harnessing the full potential of generative AI.

10. Network with AI Professionals

Connect with professionals who specialize in generative AI or AI applications in your field. Networking can lead to valuable insights, collaborations, and opportunities to learn from experts in the field.

11. Evaluate ROI

Measure the return on investment (ROI) of using generative AI in your career. Assess whether the time and resources spent on AI adoption lead to tangible benefits such as increased productivity, improved decision-making, or enhanced creativity.

12. Share Your Knowledge

If you become proficient in using generative AI to upskill your career, consider sharing your knowledge with others. Writing articles, giving presentations, or mentoring colleagues can help you solidify your expertise and contribute to the broader AI community. Generative AI is a dynamic and transformative tool that can empower you to excel in your career. By following these tips and staying open to innovation, you can leverage the capabilities of generative AI to enhance your skills, drive efficiency, and achieve new heights in your professional journey. Embrace the future of AI, and let it be your partner in career growth and success.

Generative AI is a powerful tool that can help you to upskill your career in a number of ways. Here are some of the key takeaways from this chapter:

Generative AI can be used to learn new skills, create content, automate tasks, and collaborate with others.

There are many different generative AI tools available, so it is important to choose the right one for your specific needs.

Start with simple tasks and experiment with different settings to learn how to use generative AI effectively.

Be creative and explore different ways to use generative AI to upskill your career.

Monitor your results and identify any areas where you need to improve.

Resources for learning more about generative AI

Here are some resources where you can learn more about generative AI:

Books:

Generative AI: A Practical Guide by Esteban Garcia-Ril

Generative Deep Learning: A Hands-on Guide by David Foster

Generative Adversarial Networks: A Beginner's Guide by Yaroslav Ganin

Websites:

Google AI Blog: https://ai.googleblog.com/

OpenAI Blog: https://openai.com/blog/

Papers with Code: https://paperswithcode.com/

Online courses:

Coursera: https://www.coursera.org/

Udemy: https://www.udemy.com/

edX: https://www.edx.org/

Different ways to upskill for AI careers

There are many different ways to upskill for AI careers. Here are a few options:

Online learning resources: There are many online learning resources available that can teach you the skills you need for an AI career. For example, you can take online courses in machine learning, deep learning, and natural language processing.

Bootcamps and certification programs: There are also bootcamps and certification programs that can teach you the skills you need for an AI career. These programs are typically more intensive than online learning resources, but they can also prepare you for a job in AI more quickly.

University programs: If you want to pursue a career in AI research or engineering, you may want to consider getting a university degree in computer science or a related field.

Generative AI is a rapidly growing field with the potential to revolutionize many industries and professions. By upskilling in generative AI, you can make yourself more competitive in the job market and increase your chances of success in the future of work.

Chapter 6: Upskilling Using Machine Learning

What is machine learning?
Machine learning is a type of artificial intelligence (AI) that allows software applications to become more accurate in predicting outcomes without being explicitly programmed to do so. Machine learning algorithms use historical data as input to predict new output values.
Why is upskilling in machine learning important?
Machine learning is one of the most in-demand skills in the world today. As businesses increasingly rely on data to make decisions, they need employees who can understand and apply machine learning techniques. Upskilling in machine learning can make you more competitive in the job market and open up new opportunities for career advancement.
How can machine learning be used to upskill your career?
Machine learning can be used to upskill your career in a number of ways. For example, you can use machine learning to:
Learn new skills. Machine learning can be used to learn a variety of new skills, such as programming, data science, and marketing.
Automate tasks. Machine learning can be used to automate a variety of tasks, such as data entry, customer service, and social media marketing. This can free up your time so that you can focus on more important tasks.
Improve your decision-making. Machine learning can be used to improve your decision-making by providing you with insights into your data. For example, you can use machine learning to predict customer behavior or identify trends in your sales data.
Create new products and services. Machine learning can be used to create new products and services that are tailored to the needs of your customers. For example, you can use machine learning to

recommend products to customers or to develop personalized marketing campaigns.

Here are a few examples of how machine learning is being used to upskill people in different careers:

Software engineers: Machine learning is being used to develop new software applications and to improve existing ones. For example, machine learning is being used to develop self-driving cars and to improve the accuracy of medical diagnosis systems.

Data scientists: Machine learning is being used to analyze data and extract insights from it. For example, data scientists are using machine learning to analyze customer data to identify trends and patterns.

Product managers: Machine learning is being used to develop new products and services that are tailored to the needs of customers. For example, product managers are using machine learning to recommend products to customers and to develop personalized marketing campaigns.

Marketers: Machine learning is being used to target marketing campaigns and to measure their effectiveness. For example, marketers are using machine learning to identify potential customers and to develop personalized marketing campaigns.

Salespeople: Machine learning is being used to identify potential leads and to qualify them. For example, salespeople are using machine learning to identify potential customers who are most likely to be interested in their product or service.

Customer service representatives: Machine learning is being used to automate customer service tasks and to provide customers with personalized support. For example, customer service representatives are using machine learning to answer customer questions and to resolve customer issues.

If you are interested in upskilling in machine learning, there are a number of resources available to you. You can take online courses, attend bootcamps, or pursue a certification program. There are also many books and websites that can teach you about machine learning.

By upskilling in machine learning, you can make yourself more competitive in the job market and open up new opportunities for career advancement.

Types of machine learning

There are three main types of machine learning: supervised learning, unsupervised learning, and reinforcement learning.

Supervised learning

Supervised learning is a type of machine learning where the algorithm is trained on a set of labeled data. The labeled data consists of input data and the corresponding output values. The algorithm learns to predict the output values for new input data based on the patterns it has learned from the labeled data.

Supervised learning algorithms are often used for classification and regression tasks. For example, a supervised learning algorithm could be used to classify images as containing a cat or a dog, or it could be used to predict the price of a house based on its square footage and number of bedrooms.

Unsupervised learning

Unsupervised learning is a type of machine learning where the algorithm is trained on a set of unlabeled data. The unlabeled data consists of input data but not the corresponding output values. The algorithm learns to identify patterns in the data without being explicitly told what to look for.

Unsupervised learning algorithms are often used for clustering and anomaly detection tasks. For example, an unsupervised learning algorithm could be used to cluster customers into different groups based on their purchase history, or it could be used to detect fraudulent transactions in a credit card dataset.

Reinforcement learning

Reinforcement learning is a type of machine learning where the algorithm learns to perform a task by trial and error. The algorithm is given a set of actions that it can perform and a reward signal that indicates how well it is performing. The algorithm learns to choose the actions that lead to the highest rewards.

Reinforcement learning algorithms are often used for robotics and game playing tasks. For example, a reinforcement learning algorithm could be used to train a robot to walk or to train an agent to play a video game.

Here are some examples of how the different types of machine learning are being used in the real world:

Supervised learning:

Spam filters use supervised learning to identify and block spam emails.

Product recommendation systems use supervised learning to recommend products to customers based on their purchase history.

Medical diagnosis systems use supervised learning to diagnose diseases based on patient symptoms and medical records.

Unsupervised learning:

Market segmentation algorithms use unsupervised learning to cluster customers into different groups based on their demographics and purchase behavior.

Fraud detection systems use unsupervised learning to identify fraudulent transactions in credit card datasets.

Anomalous event detection systems use unsupervised learning to identify unusual activity in networks and other systems.

Reinforcement learning:

Self-driving cars use reinforcement learning to learn how to drive safely.

Game playing agents use reinforcement learning to learn how to play games at a superhuman level.

Industrial robots use reinforcement learning to learn how to perform complex tasks.

These are just a few examples of the many ways that machine learning is being used in the real world. As machine learning continues to develop, we can expect to see even more innovative and groundbreaking applications in the future.

Machine learning skills for different careers

Machine learning is a valuable skill for many different careers. Here are some examples of machine learning skills that are in demand in different industries:

Software engineering

Software engineers who have machine learning skills are in high demand. These engineers can develop new machine learning algorithms and apply them to solve real-world problems. They may also work on developing machine learning tools and frameworks.

Data science

Data scientists use machine learning algorithms to analyze data and extract insights from it. They may also develop and deploy machine learning models to production.

Product management

Product managers who have machine learning skills can use these skills to develop new products and features that are tailored to the needs of their customers. They may also use machine learning to analyze customer data and identify trends.

Marketing

Marketers who have machine learning skills can use these skills to target their marketing campaigns more effectively. They may also use machine learning to measure the effectiveness of their campaigns and to identify new opportunities.

Sales

Salespeople who have machine learning skills can use these skills to identify potential leads and to qualify them. They may also use machine learning to develop personalized sales pitches and to close more deals.

Customer service

Customer service representatives who have machine learning skills can use these skills to provide customers with more personalized support. They may also use machine learning to automate customer service tasks and to resolve customer issues more quickly.

Here are some specific examples of how machine learning skills can be used in different careers:

- A software engineer at a tech company could use machine learning to develop a new algorithm for recommending products to customers.
- A data scientist at a healthcare company could use machine learning to analyze patient data and identify patterns that could lead to new treatments for diseases.
- A product manager at a social media company could use machine learning to develop new features that are tailored to the interests of its users.
- A marketer at a retail company could use machine learning to target its marketing campaigns to customers who are most likely to be interested in its products.
- A salesperson at a software company could use machine learning to identify potential leads and to qualify them.
- A customer service representative at a bank could use machine learning to automate tasks such as answering customer questions and resolving customer issues.

By developing your machine learning skills, you can make yourself more competitive in the job market and open up new opportunities for career advancement.

How to Upskill in Machine Learning

Machine learning is at the forefront of the technological revolution, with applications spanning various industries. Whether you're looking to advance your current career or embark on a new one, upskilling in machine learning can be a game-changer. In this chapter, we'll explore various avenues for acquiring machine learning skills and expertise.

Online Courses

Online courses are an excellent way to start your journey into machine learning. Platforms like Coursera, edX, Udemy, and Khan

Academy offer a wide range of courses catering to all skill levels. Here's how to make the most of online courses:

Choose the Right Course: Begin with foundational courses if you're new to machine learning. For those with some experience, opt for intermediate or advanced courses.

Diversify Your Learning: Explore different courses from multiple providers to gain a well-rounded understanding of machine learning techniques.

Practice What You Learn: Apply your knowledge by working on real-world projects and exercises provided in the courses.

Bootcamps

Bootcamps offer immersive, intensive training in machine learning. They are ideal for individuals who want to upskill quickly and are willing to commit to an intensive learning schedule. Key points to consider when enrolling in a bootcamp:

Duration and Intensity: Bootcamps can range from a few weeks to several months. Choose one that aligns with your availability and commitment level.

Hands-on Experience: Look for bootcamps that provide hands-on projects and opportunities to collaborate with peers.

Career Support: Some bootcamps offer career services such as job placement assistance and networking opportunities.

Certifications

Certifications can validate your machine learning skills and make your resume stand out. Consider the following certification options:

Google Cloud Professional Machine Learning Engineer: For those interested in deploying machine learning models in the cloud.

Microsoft Certified: Azure AI Engineer Associate: Focuses on building, training, and deploying AI solutions on Microsoft Azure.

Coursera Specializations: Platforms like Coursera offer specialization certificates from top universities in machine learning and related fields.

Self-Study

Self-study is a flexible and cost-effective way to learn machine learning. While it requires discipline and self-motivation, it can be highly rewarding. Here are some self-study strategies:

Textbooks and Documentation: Start with textbooks like "Pattern Recognition and Machine Learning" by Christopher M. Bishop or explore documentation from machine learning libraries like TensorFlow and scikit-learn.

Online Resources: Utilize online tutorials, blogs, and forums to find solutions to problems and stay updated on the latest developments.

Hands-on Projects: Apply what you learn by working on personal machine learning projects or contributing to open-source projects.

Networking and Collaboration

Networking and collaboration are vital in the field of machine learning. Here's how to maximize your opportunities:

Join Online Communities: Participate in online forums, LinkedIn groups, and social media communities focused on machine learning. Engaging with peers can provide insights and potential collaborations.

Attend Meetups and Conferences: Attend local meetups and conferences related to machine learning to connect with professionals and stay current with industry trends.

Collaborate on Projects: Collaborative projects provide practical experience and allow you to learn from others in the field.

Upskilling in machine learning is an investment in your future, offering opportunities for career growth and innovation. Whether you prefer structured courses, immersive bootcamps, certifications, or self-study, the key is to stay committed, practice consistently, and engage with the machine learning community. As you gain expertise, you'll be well-equipped to tackle real-world challenges and contribute to the exciting developments in this ever-evolving field.

Resources for learning machine learning

There are a number of resources available to help you learn machine learning. Here are a few examples:

Books

Machine Learning: A Probabilistic Perspective by Kevin P. Murphy

An Introduction to Statistical Learning: With Applications in R by Gareth James, Daniela Witten, Trevor Hastie, and Robert Tibshirani

Hands-On Machine Learning with Scikit-Learn, Keras, and TensorFlow by Aurélien Géron

Deep Learning by Ian Goodfellow, Yoshua Bengio, and Aaron Courville

Machine Learning Yearning by Andrew Ng

Websites

Google AI Blog (https://ai.googleblog.com/)

OpenAI Blog (https://openai.com/blog/)

Papers with Code (https://paperswithcode.com/)

Machine Learning Mastery (https://www.machinelearningmastery.com/)

Towards Data Science (https://towardsdatascience.com/)

Online courses

Machine Learning by Andrew Ng on Coursera
Deep Learning by Geoffrey Hinton on Coursera
Introduction to Machine Learning by Sebastian Thrun on Udacity
Machine Learning by Georgia Tech on Udacity
Deep Learning by Vincent Vanhoucke on Udacity
Bootcamps
General Assembly
Flatiron School
Hack Reactor
Metis
Springboard
Certifications
Google Cloud Certified Professional Cloud Machine Learning Engineer
AWS Certified Machine Learning Specialty
Microsoft Certified: Azure Solutions Architect Expert
IBM Certified Data Scientist - Professional
Stanford Certificate in Data Science
These are just a few examples of the many resources available to help you learn machine learning. When choosing resources, it is important to consider your learning style and your budget.

If you are new to machine learning, I recommend starting with a book or online course that provides a general overview of the subject. Once you have a basic understanding of machine learning, you can start to learn more about specific machine learning algorithms and techniques.

If you are interested in pursuing a career in machine learning, I recommend attending a bootcamp or getting a certification. These programs can help you learn the skills you need to be successful in a machine learning career.

No matter which resources you choose, it is important to be patient and persistent when learning machine learning. It takes time and effort to master this complex subject. But with hard work and dedication, you can achieve your machine learning goals.

Chapter 7: Upskilling By Learning Python

Getting started with Python for AI and ML
To get started with Python for AI and ML, you will need to install Python and the necessary libraries. You can download Python from the official Python website: https://www.python.org/downloads/. Once you have installed Python, you can install the necessary libraries using the pip package manager.
Here are some of the most important libraries for AI and ML:
NumPy: NumPy is a library for scientific computing with Python. It provides support for large, multi-dimensional arrays and matrices, along with a large collection of mathematical functions.
Pandas: Pandas is a library for data analysis and manipulation with Python. It provides data structures and operations for working with tabular data, such as DataFrames and Series.
scikit-learn: scikit-learn is a library for machine learning in Python. It provides a wide range of machine learning algorithms for classification, regression, clustering, and dimensionality reduction.
TensorFlow: TensorFlow is a library for deep learning in Python. It is used to train and deploy deep learning models, such as neural networks.
PyTorch: PyTorch is another popular library for deep learning in Python. It is known for its flexibility and ease of use.
Once you have installed Python and the necessary libraries, you can start setting up your development environment. This may involve installing a code editor or IDE, such as Visual Studio Code or PyCharm. You may also want to set up a virtual environment to manage your Python packages.
To write basic Python code, you will need to learn about Python data types, variables, functions, control flow, and object-oriented programming. There are many resources available online and in libraries that can teach you the basics of Python programming.
Here is a simple example of a Python program:

```python
# Print "Hello, world!" to the console.
print("Hello, world!")
```

To run this program, you would save it as a file with a .py extension, such as hello_world.py, and then run it in a terminal or command prompt.

Once you have learned the basics of Python programming, you can start learning about more advanced topics such as data structures and algorithms, machine learning, and deep learning.

Python basics for AI and ML

Python is a general-purpose programming language that is used for a wide variety of tasks, including web development, data science, and machine learning. It is a popular choice for beginners because it is easy to learn and use.

Here are some of the reasons why you should learn Python:

Python is easy to learn: Python has a simple syntax that is easy to read and write. This makes it a good choice for beginners who are just starting to learn programming.

Python is versatile: Python can be used for a wide variety of tasks, including web development, data science, and machine learning. This makes it a good choice for people who want to learn a language that can be used for a variety of different projects.

Python has a large community: Python has a large and active community of developers. This means that there are many resources available to help you learn Python and to get help with problems that you may encounter.

Python is the primary programming language for AI and ML: Python is the most popular programming language for AI and ML. If you want to learn AI and ML, then learning Python is a must.

Here are some specific examples of how Python is used in AI and ML:

Developing and training machine learning models: Python is used to develop and train a wide variety of machine learning models, such as neural networks, decision trees, and support vector machines.

Processing and analyzing data: Python is used to process and analyze data for AI and ML projects. This includes tasks such as cleaning and preprocessing data, feature engineering, and data visualization.

Deploying and maintaining AI and ML systems: Python is used to deploy and maintain AI and ML systems to production environments.

If you are interested in learning AI and ML, then learning Python is a great place to start. Python is a powerful language that can be used to develop and deploy AI and ML systems of all sizes.

Here is a brief overview of some of the most important Python basics for AI and ML:

Python data types

Python has a number of built-in data types, including:

- Integers: Integers are whole numbers, such as 1, 2, and 3.
- Floats: Floats are decimal numbers, such as 1.5 and 2.5.
- Strings: Strings are sequences of characters, such as "Hello, world!" and "This is a string."
- Booleans: Booleans are values that can be either True or False.

Python also supports more complex data types, such as lists, dictionaries, and sets. Lists are ordered collections of elements, dictionaries are unordered collections of key-value pairs, and sets are unordered collections of unique elements.

Python variables

Python variables are used to store data. To create a variable, you simply assign a value to it. For example:

```python
Python
# Create a variable called "name" and assign it the value "Richard".
name = "Richard"
# Print the value of the variable "name" to the console.
print(name)
```

Python functions

Python functions are used to group code together and perform a specific task. To define a function, you use the def keyword. For example:

```python
# Define a function called "greet()".
def greet(name):
  """Greets the user by name."""
```

```
  print(f"Hello, {name}!")
# Call the "greet()" function.
greet(name)
```

Python control flow
Python control flow statements allow you to control the flow of
execution of your program. The most common control flow
statements are if , elif , and else .
For example, the following code will print "Hello, world!" if the
variable x is equal to 1:

```
x = 1
if x == 1:
  print("Hello, world!")
```

Python object-oriented programming
Python is an object-oriented programming language. This means
that you can create classes and objects. Classes are blueprints for
objects, and objects are instances of classes.
For example, the following code defines a class called Person :

```
Python
class Person:
  """A class to represent a person."""
  def __init__(self, name):
    self.name = name
  def greet(self):
    """Greets the user by name."""
    print(f"Hello, my name is {self.name}!")
# Create an instance of the `Person` class.
person = Person("Richard")
# Call the "greet()" method on the `person` object.
person.greet()
```

This is just a brief overview of some of the most important Python
basics for AI and ML. There are many other topics that you will need
to learn, such as data structures and algorithms, machine learning,
and deep learning. However, this overview should give you a good
foundation to start from.

Python data structures and algorithms for AI and ML

Python data structures and algorithms are essential for AI and ML. Data structures are used to store and organize data, while algorithms are used to process and analyze data.

Here is a brief overview of some of the most important Python data structures and algorithms for AI and ML:

Python lists

Python lists are ordered collections of elements. Lists can contain elements of any type, including integers, floats, strings, and other lists.

Lists are useful for storing data that needs to be accessed in order. For example, you could use a list to store the names of your customers or the prices of your products.

Python dictionaries

Python dictionaries are unordered collections of key-value pairs. Dictionaries can store keys and values of any type.

Dictionaries are useful for storing data that needs to be accessed by key. For example, you could use a dictionary to store the user accounts on your website or the product reviews on your e-commerce site.

Python sets

Python sets are unordered collections of unique elements. Sets can store elements of any type.

Sets are useful for storing data that needs to be unique. For example, you could use a set to store the unique products that a customer has purchased or the unique users that have visited your website.

NumPy arrays

NumPy arrays are multi-dimensional arrays that are optimized for scientific computing. NumPy arrays can store elements of any numeric type, such as integers, floats, and complex numbers. NumPy arrays are essential for many AI and ML tasks, such as machine learning model training and evaluation.

Machine learning algorithms

There are many different machine learning algorithms that can be implemented in Python. Some of the most common machine learning algorithms include:

Linear regression: Linear regression is a machine learning algorithm that is used to predict continuous values, such as the price of a house or the number of visitors to a website.

Logistic regression: Logistic regression is a machine learning algorithm that is used to predict binary values, such as whether or not a customer will churn or whether or not an email is spam.

Decision trees: Decision trees are machine learning algorithms that are used to predict both continuous and binary values. Decision trees are easy to understand and interpret, which makes them a popular choice for many AI and ML tasks.

Support vector machines (SVMs): SVMs are machine learning algorithms that are used to classify data. SVMs are known for their accuracy and generalization performance.

Random forests: Random forests are machine learning algorithms that are used for both classification and regression. Random forests are ensembles of decision trees, which makes them more robust and accurate than individual decision trees.

These are just a few examples of the many Python data structures and algorithms that can be used for AI and ML. There are many other resources available online and in libraries that can teach you more about these topics.

I encourage you to explore these resources and start learning today!

Python libraries and frameworks for AI and ML

There are many popular Python libraries and frameworks for AI and ML. Some of the most popular include:

TensorFlow

TensorFlow is a library for deep learning in Python. It is used to train and deploy deep learning models, such as neural networks. TensorFlow is developed by Google and is used by many companies and organizations, including Google, Facebook, and Amazon.

PyTorch

PyTorch is another popular library for deep learning in Python. It is known for its flexibility and ease of use. PyTorch is developed by Facebook and is used by many companies and organizations, including Facebook, Google, and Microsoft.

scikit-learn

scikit-learn is a library for machine learning in Python. It provides a wide range of machine learning algorithms for classification, regression, clustering, and dimensionality reduction. scikit-learn is developed by a community of volunteers and is used by many companies and organizations, including Google, Facebook, and Microsoft.

Other popular Python libraries and frameworks for AI and ML include:

Keras: Keras is a high-level API for TensorFlow and PyTorch. It makes it easier to build and train deep learning models.

OpenCV: OpenCV is a library for computer vision in Python. It provides a wide range of functions for image processing, video processing, and machine learning.

Matplotlib: Matplotlib is a library for data visualization in Python. It provides a wide range of functions for creating charts, graphs, and plots.

NumPy: NumPy is a library for scientific computing in Python. It provides support for large, multi-dimensional arrays and matrices, along with a large collection of mathematical functions.

These are just a few of the many Python libraries and frameworks that are available for AI and ML. When choosing a library or framework, it is important to consider your needs and the specific tasks that you want to accomplish.

I encourage you to explore the different libraries and frameworks that are available and choose the ones that are right for you.

Python for AI model development

To develop AI models in Python, you will need to learn how to load and prepare data, train and evaluate machine learning models, and save and deploy machine learning models.

Loading and preparing data

The first step in developing an AI model is to load and prepare the data. This involves loading the data from a data source, such as a CSV file or a database, and then cleaning and transforming the data into a format that can be used by the machine learning algorithm.

There are many Python libraries that can be used for data loading and preparation. Some of the most popular libraries include:

Pandas: Pandas is a library for data analysis and manipulation with Python. It provides data structures and operations for working with tabular data, such as DataFrames and Series.

NumPy: NumPy is a library for scientific computing with Python. It provides support for large, multi-dimensional arrays and matrices, along with a large collection of mathematical functions.

scikit-learn: scikit-learn also provides a number of functions for data preprocessing, such as feature scaling and one-hot encoding.

Training and evaluating machine learning models

Once you have loaded and prepared the data, you can start training the machine learning model. This involves feeding the data to the machine learning algorithm and allowing the algorithm to learn from the data.

There are many different machine learning algorithms that can be used for different tasks. Some of the most common machine learning algorithms include:

Linear regression: Linear regression is a machine learning algorithm that is used to predict continuous values, such as the price of a house or the number of visitors to a website.

Logistic regression: Logistic regression is a machine learning algorithm that is used to predict binary values, such as whether or not a customer will churn or whether or not an email is spam.

Decision trees: Decision trees are machine learning algorithms that are used to predict both continuous and binary values. Decision trees are easy to understand and interpret, which makes them a popular choice for many AI and ML tasks.

Support vector machines (SVMs): SVMs are machine learning algorithms that are used to classify data. SVMs are known for their accuracy and generalization performance.

Random forests: Random forests are machine learning algorithms that are used for both classification and regression. Random forests are ensembles of decision trees, which makes them more robust and accurate than individual decision trees.

Once you have trained the machine learning model, you need to evaluate the model to see how well it performs on new data. This can be done by splitting the data into a training set and a test set. The training set is used to train the model, and the test set is used to evaluate the model.

Saving and deploying machine learning models

Once you are satisfied with the performance of the machine learning model, you can save the model to a file. This allows you to deploy the model to production and use it to make predictions on new data.

There are many different ways to deploy machine learning models in production. One common approach is to use a web service. A web service is a software application that can be accessed over the internet. You can deploy your machine learning model to a web service and then use the web service to make predictions on new data.

Another common approach is to deploy a machine learning model to a mobile device. This allows you to make predictions on new data without having to connect to a server.

Once you have deployed the machine learning model, you can start using it to make predictions on new data. This can be done by feeding the new data to the model and the model will return a prediction.

Python for ML model deployment

Once you have trained and evaluated your machine learning model, you need to deploy it to production so that it can be used to make predictions on new data. There are a number of ways to deploy machine learning models, and the best approach for you will depend on your specific needs and requirements.

One common approach to deploying machine learning models is to use a web server. A web server is a software application that can be accessed over the internet. You can deploy your machine learning model to a web server and then use the web server to make predictions on new data.

To deploy a machine learning model to a web server, you will need to create a web service API. A web service API is a set of rules that define how the web service interacts with other applications.

There are a number of Python libraries that can be used to create web service APIs. Some of the most popular libraries include:

Flask: Flask is a lightweight web framework for Python. It is easy to use and can be used to create complex web applications.

Django: Django is a full-featured web framework for Python. It is more complex to use than Flask, but it provides a number of features that are not available in Flask, such as support for user authentication and authorization.

Once you have created a web service API, you need to deploy the web service to a production environment. There are a number of cloud platforms that can be used to deploy web services, such as Amazon Web Services (AWS), Microsoft Azure, and Google Cloud Platform (GCP).

Another common approach to deploying machine learning models is to use a cloud platform. Cloud platforms provide a variety of services that can be used to deploy and manage machine learning models.

For example, AWS provides a service called Amazon SageMaker. Amazon SageMaker provides a number of features that make it easy to deploy and manage machine learning models in the cloud, such as pre-built machine learning algorithms, pre-configured machine learning environments, and managed machine learning model deployment.

Once you have deployed your machine learning model to production, you can start using it to make predictions on new data. This can be done by sending a request to the web service API or by using the cloud platform's machine learning service.

Here are some additional tips for deploying machine learning models in Python:

Use a model management framework. A model management framework can help you to track and manage your machine learning models in production. Some popular model management frameworks include MLflow and Kubeflow.

Use a continuous integration/continuous delivery (CI/CD) pipeline. A CI/CD pipeline can help you to automate the process of building, testing, and deploying your machine learning models.

Monitor your models in production. It is important to monitor your machine learning models in production to ensure that they are performing as expected. You can use a monitoring tool to track the performance of your models and to identify any potential problems.

Python for AI and ML research

Python is a popular language for AI and ML research because it is easy to learn and use, and it has a large and active community of developers. Python also has a number of libraries and frameworks that are specifically designed for AI and ML research.

Here are some tips on how to use Python for AI and ML research:

- Use a Python environment manager. A Python environment manager can help you to create and manage different Python environments for different AI and ML research projects. Some popular Python environment managers include conda and virtualenv.
- Use a Python library for machine learning. There are a number of Python libraries that can be used for machine learning research. Some popular libraries include scikit-learn, TensorFlow, and PyTorch.
- Use a Python library for data analysis and visualization. There are a number of Python libraries that can be used for data analysis and visualization. Some popular libraries include Pandas, NumPy, and Matplotlib.
- Use a Python library for scientific computing. There are a number of Python libraries that can be used for scientific computing. Some popular libraries include NumPy and SciPy.

Python for AI and ML engineering

AI and ML engineering is the process of developing, deploying, and maintaining AI and ML systems. Python is a popular language for AI and ML engineering because it is easy to learn and use, and it has a large and active community of developers. Python also has a number of libraries and frameworks that are specifically designed for AI and ML engineering.

Here are some tips on how to use Python for AI and ML engineering:

Use a Python framework for machine learning. There are a number of Python frameworks that can be used for machine learning engineering. Some popular frameworks include TensorFlow Serving, PyTorch Serving, and Kubeflow Pipelines.

Use a Python library for cloud computing. There are a number of Python libraries that can be used for cloud computing. Some popular libraries include boto3 for AWS, Azure SDK for Python for Azure, and google-cloud-python for GCP.

Use a Python library for data engineering. There are a number of Python libraries that can be used for data engineering. Some popular libraries include Apache Spark and Apache Airflow.

Here are some examples of how Python can be used for AI and ML engineering:

- Developing and deploying machine learning pipelines: Python can be used to develop and deploy machine learning pipelines. A machine learning pipeline is a series of steps that are used to train, deploy, and monitor a machine learning model.
- Developing and deploying recommendation systems: Python can be used to develop and deploy recommendation systems. A recommendation system is a system that recommends products, services, or content to users based on their past behavior or preferences.
- Monitoring and maintaining AI and ML systems: Python can be used to monitor and maintain AI and ML systems. This includes monitoring the performance of the systems, identifying and troubleshooting problems, and retraining the models as needed.

Chapter 8: They Took 'Er Jerbs, Industries and Skills Most Likely To Be Impacted By AI

Artificial intelligence (AI) is rapidly transforming the world of work. From the assembly line to the doctor's office, AI is automating tasks and processes that were once done by humans. This is raising concerns about job displacement and the future of work.

However, it is important to remember that AI is also creating new jobs and opportunities. As AI-powered systems become more sophisticated, they will require new skills to develop, maintain, and operate them. Additionally, AI will create new industries and markets that we cannot even imagine today.

In this chapter, we will explore the impact of AI on jobs from both perspectives. We will discuss the industries and skills that are most likely to be impacted by AI, as well as the new jobs and opportunities that AI is creating. We will also provide tips on how to prepare for the future of work in the age of AI.

Key questions to be addressed in the chapter:

What are the different ways that AI is impacting jobs?

Which industries and skills are most likely to be impacted by AI?

What new jobs and opportunities is AI creating?

How can we prepare for the future of work in the age of AI?

Industries most likely to be impacted by AI

The industries that are most likely to be impacted by AI are those that involve repetitive tasks and processes. These industries include:

- Manufacturing: AI is already being used to automate many manufacturing tasks, such as assembly, welding, and painting. In the future, AI is expected to automate even more manufacturing tasks, such as product design and quality control.
- Transportation: AI is being used to develop self-driving cars and trucks, which could revolutionize the transportation industry. AI is also being used to improve traffic management and to develop new transportation systems, such as hyperloop.

- Healthcare: AI is being used to diagnose diseases, develop treatments, and provide patient care. AI is also being used to develop new medical devices and drugs.
- Finance: AI is being used to automate trading, detect fraud, and manage risk. AI is also being used to develop new financial products and services.
- Customer service: AI is being used to develop chatbots and virtual assistants that can provide customer support. AI is also being used to analyze customer data and to predict customer needs.
- Retail: AI is being used to recommend products to customers, predict demand, and manage inventory. AI is also being used to develop new retail experiences, such as augmented reality shopping.

In addition to these industries, AI is also expected to have a significant impact on many other industries, such as education, law, and media.

It is important to note that AI is not expected to replace all jobs in these industries. However, AI is expected to automate many routine tasks, which could lead to job displacement for some workers. It is also important to note that AI is creating new jobs, such as AI engineers and data scientists.

Overall, AI is expected to have a significant impact on the world of work. It is important to be aware of the changes that AI is bringing about and to be prepared to adapt.

Skills most likely to be replaced by AI

The skills that are most likely to be replaced by AI are those that are repetitive and routine. These skills include:

- Data entry: AI is already being used to automate data entry tasks, such as entering data into spreadsheets and databases. AI is expected to automate even more data entry tasks in the future.
- Customer service: AI is being used to develop chatbots and virtual assistants that can provide customer support. AI is expected to automate even more customer service tasks in the future.
- Manufacturing jobs: AI is being used to automate many manufacturing tasks, such as assembly, welding, and painting. AI is expected to automate even more manufacturing tasks in the future.
- Transportation jobs: AI is being used to develop self-driving cars and trucks, which could revolutionize the transportation

industry. AI is expected to automate many transportation jobs, such as truck driving and taxi driving.

- Retail jobs: AI is being used to develop self-checkout systems and to recommend products to customers. AI is expected to automate many retail jobs, such as cashier and sales associate.

In addition to these skills, AI is also expected to automate many other skills, such as accounting, legal research, and medical diagnosis.

It is important to note that AI is not expected to replace all jobs. However, AI is expected to automate many routine tasks, which could lead to job displacement for some workers. It is also important to note that AI is creating new jobs, such as AI engineers and data scientists.

Overall, AI is expected to have a significant impact on the world of work. It is important to be aware of the changes that AI is bringing about and to be prepared to adapt.

How to prepare for the future of work in the age of AI

There are a number of things that you can do to prepare for the future of work in the age of AI:

- Develop your skills in areas that are less likely to be automated: This includes skills such as creativity, problem-solving, and communication.
- Learn about AI: The more you know about AI, the better prepared you will be for the changes that it is bringing about.
- Be adaptable: Be prepared to adapt to new technologies and new ways of working.
- Be a lifelong learner: The world is changing rapidly, and so should you. Be willing to learn new things throughout your career.

By following these tips, you can thrive in the future of work.

Skills that will be in demand in the age of AI

Even though AI is automating some jobs, it is also creating new jobs that require new skills. The skills that will be in demand in the age of AI include:

Programming: Programming is the essential skill for developing and maintaining AI systems. AI engineers use programming languages such as Python, R, and TensorFlow to develop and train AI models.

Data science: Data science is the field of extracting knowledge from data. Data scientists use data science tools and techniques to prepare, clean, and analyze data to identify patterns and trends.

This information can then be used to improve AI models and develop new AI products and services.

Machine learning: Machine learning is a subset of AI that allows computers to learn without being explicitly programmed. Machine learning engineers use machine learning techniques to develop AI models that can learn from data and make predictions.

Creativity: AI is still in its early stages of development, and there is a lot of room for creativity in the field. Creative AI professionals are developing new ways to use AI to solve problems and improve people's lives.

Problem-solving: AI is often used to solve complex problems. AI professionals need to be able to identify problems, develop solutions, and test and evaluate their solutions.

Communication: AI professionals need to be able to communicate effectively with both technical and non-technical audiences. They need to be able to explain complex concepts in a clear and concise way.

These skills are essential for developing and maintaining AI systems. They are also important for working in other fields that are being impacted by AI, such as healthcare, finance, and manufacturing.

If you are interested in a career in AI, I recommend that you develop your skills in these areas. You can do this by taking online courses, reading books and articles, and attending conferences and workshops. You can also gain experience by working on personal projects or contributing to open source AI projects.

The future of work is rapidly changing, but AI is sure to play a major role. By developing the skills that will be in demand in the age of AI, you can position yourself for success in the years to come.

Chapter 9: The Meaning of Work

The meaning of work is a complex and philosophical question that has been pondered by humans for centuries. There is no one answer that will satisfy everyone, as the meaning of work is a personal and individual journey. However, there are some common themes that emerge when considering the meaning of work.

Work is often seen as a source of income, identity, and meaning. It can provide us with the financial resources we need to meet our basic needs and live a comfortable life. It can also give us a sense of purpose and belonging, and help us to define who we are as individuals.

What is the meaning of work?

The meaning of work can be different for everyone. For some people, work is simply a means to an end. It is a way to earn money and support themselves and their families. For others, work is a more fundamental part of their lives. It is a way to express their creativity, make a difference in the world, and connect with others.

There is no right or wrong answer to the question of what the meaning of work is. The important thing is to find work that is meaningful to you. This may mean finding work that aligns with your values and interests, or work that allows you to make a positive impact on the world.

Why is the meaning of work important?

The meaning of work is important because it can have a significant impact on our overall well-being. When we find work that is meaningful to us, we are more likely to be engaged and motivated. We are also more likely to feel satisfied with our lives and have a sense of purpose.

On the other hand, when we work in jobs that we find meaningless or unfulfilling, we are more likely to experience stress, burnout, and dissatisfaction. This can lead to a number of negative consequences, such as health problems, relationship problems, and decreased productivity.

How is the meaning of work changing in the age of AI?

The rise of artificial intelligence (AI) is having a major impact on the world of work. AI is automating many jobs, and the nature of work is changing rapidly. This is raising questions about the future of work and the meaning of work in the age of AI.

One of the biggest concerns is that AI will lead to mass unemployment. As AI automates more and more jobs, people will be left jobless. This could lead to a decline in living standards and social unrest.

Another concern is that the rise of the gig economy will make it more difficult for people to find meaningful work. In the gig economy, people work temporary jobs or freelance work. This type of work can be unstable and unpredictable. It can also be difficult to find meaningful work in the gig economy.

Finally, the changing nature of work is also raising questions about the meaning of work. In the past, work was often seen as a source of identity and purpose. However, as AI automates more and more jobs, it is becoming more difficult to find meaning in work.

The meaning of work is changing in the age of AI. AI is automating many jobs, and the nature of work is changing rapidly. This raises questions about the future of work and the meaning of work in the age of AI.

It is important to think about how you can find meaning in work in the age of AI. You may need to develop new skills or find new ways to find meaning in work. It is also important to be adaptable and willing to change. The world of work is changing rapidly, and you need to be able to change with it.

The traditional meaning of work

The traditional meaning of work has been shaped by centuries of industrialization and capitalism. In the traditional view, work is seen as a necessary evil. It is something that people have to do in order to earn money and survive.

Work is also seen as a source of identity. People define themselves by their jobs. Their jobs give them a sense of purpose and belonging.

Finally, work is seen as a source of meaning and purpose. People find meaning in their work when they feel like they are making a contribution to the world and that their work is worthwhile.

Work as a source of income

Work is a primary source of income for most people. It is how people earn the money they need to meet their basic needs and live a comfortable life.

Work provides people with the financial resources they need to buy food, shelter, clothing, and other necessities. It also allows people to save money for the future and invest in their education and retirement.

Work as a source of identity

People often define themselves by their jobs. Their jobs give them a sense of purpose and belonging.

Work can also provide people with a sense of accomplishment and self-worth. When people are good at their jobs and they feel like they are making a difference, they feel good about themselves.

Work as a source of meaning and purpose

People find meaning in their work when they feel like they are making a contribution to the world and that their work is worthwhile. Work can give people a sense of purpose and direction in their lives. It can also help them to connect with others and build relationships.

The traditional meaning of work is complex and multifaceted. Work is seen as a source of income, identity, and meaning and purpose. However, the meaning of work is changing in the age of AI. AI is automating many jobs, and the nature of work is changing rapidly. This is raising questions about the future of work and the meaning of work in the age of AI.

The changing meaning of work in the age of AI

The rise of artificial intelligence (AI) is having a major impact on the world of work. AI is automating many jobs, and the nature of work is changing rapidly. This is raising questions about the future of work and the meaning of work in the age of AI.

The automation of jobs

One of the biggest concerns about AI is that it will lead to mass unemployment. As AI automates more and more jobs, people will be left jobless. This could lead to a decline in living standards and social unrest.

AI is already automating many jobs in a variety of industries, including manufacturing, healthcare, finance, and customer service. For example, AI-powered robots are now being used to assemble cars, diagnose diseases, and provide customer support.

It is difficult to predict how many jobs will be automated by AI in the future. However, some experts believe that up to 50% of all jobs could be automated in the next few decades.

The rise of the gig economy

Another trend that is changing the meaning of work is the rise of the gig economy. The gig economy is a labor market in which people work temporary jobs or freelance work instead of full-time jobs.

The gig economy is growing rapidly, and it is now estimated that over 30% of the workforce in the United States is working in the gig economy.

The gig economy offers a number of benefits, such as flexibility and autonomy. However, it also presents a number of challenges, such as lack of job security and benefits.

The rise of AI and the gig economy is changing the meaning of work in a number of ways. AI is automating many jobs, and the gig economy is making it more difficult for people to find meaningful work.

This is raising questions about how people will find meaning and purpose in the age of AI. It is important to think about how you can prepare for the future of work and how you can find meaning in work in the age of AI.

The Changing Nature of Work

The world of work is undergoing a profound transformation, driven by technological advancements, societal shifts, and global trends. To navigate this evolving landscape successfully, it's essential to understand not only what work will look like in the future but also how the meaning of work is being redefined.

The Future of Work

Embracing Automation and AI

Automation and artificial intelligence (AI) are reshaping industries and job roles. While they bring efficiency and innovation, they also raise questions about job displacement. In the future, repetitive and routine tasks may be automated, allowing humans to focus on creative, strategic, and uniquely human tasks that require empathy and complex problem-solving.

Gig Economy and Freelancing

The gig economy, characterized by short-term contracts and freelance work, is on the rise. This trend offers flexibility and autonomy but also challenges traditional notions of job security and benefits. In the future, more individuals may choose to work independently, with the gig economy becoming a prominent feature of the job market.

Remote and Flexible Work

Advancements in technology have made remote work more accessible. The COVID-19 pandemic accelerated this shift, leading many organizations to adopt remote and flexible work arrangements. The future of work is likely to include a blend of in-person and remote work, enabling employees to balance their professional and personal lives more effectively.

Lifelong Learning

As industries evolve rapidly, the importance of continuous learning becomes evident. The future of work will demand lifelong learning to stay relevant. Upskilling and reskilling will be essential to adapt to changing job requirements and to explore new career opportunities.

The Meaning of Work in the Future

Purpose and Impact

In the future, the meaning of work will extend beyond traditional measures of success and monetary compensation. More individuals will seek work that aligns with their values and contributes to a greater purpose. Companies that prioritize social and environmental impact will attract and retain top talent.

Hybrid Careers

The boundaries between professions will blur as individuals pursue hybrid careers that combine diverse skills and interests. The future will celebrate multidisciplinary approaches, encouraging professionals to explore intersections between technology, arts, sciences, and humanities.

Work-Life Integration

Rather than strict work-life balance, the future will emphasize work-life integration. Employees will have the autonomy to design their work schedules and environments to suit their lifestyles, resulting in increased satisfaction and productivity.

Human-Centric Leadership

Future leaders will prioritize empathy, emotional intelligence, and inclusivity. Leadership styles will shift towards a more human-centric approach, fostering collaboration, psychological safety, and well-being among employees.

Collaboration and Remote Teams

Collaboration will be a cornerstone of work in the future, enabled by technology. Cross-functional and remote teams will become the norm, transcending geographical boundaries and cultural differences.

The changing nature of work presents both challenges and opportunities. Embracing flexibility, adaptability, and a holistic view of work will be essential for individuals and organizations to thrive. As the future of work unfolds, those who can navigate these shifts while staying true to their values and aspirations will be best positioned to define their own meaningful and fulfilling careers.

How can we find meaning in work in the age of AI?

One of the most important things we can do to find meaning in work in the age of AI is to find work that is meaningful to us. This means doing work that we are passionate about and that makes a difference in the world.

It is also important to develop the skills that are in demand in the age of AI. This means developing skills such as programming, data science, and machine learning.

Finally, it is important to be adaptable and willing to change. The world of work is changing rapidly, and we need to be able to change with it. We also need to be willing to learn new things and to find meaning in work outside of our jobs.

The age of AI is bringing about many changes to the world of work. However, it is important to remember that AI is also creating new jobs and new opportunities. By following the tips above, we can find meaning in work in the age of AI.

Here are some additional thoughts on how to find meaning in work in the age of AI:

Focus on your strengths. What are you good at? What do you enjoy doing? Look for work that allows you to use your strengths and talents.

Be creative. Think about how you can use your skills and talents to make a difference in the world. There are many ways to be creative in your work, even if you are working in a traditional job.

Connect with others. Find people who share your values and interests. Build relationships with your colleagues, customers, and clients. Having strong relationships can make work more meaningful.

Give back. Find ways to give back to your community. This could involve volunteering your time, donating to charity, or simply being kind and helpful to others. Giving back can make you feel good about yourself and your work.

Remember, the meaning of work is different for everyone. What matters most is that you find work that is meaningful to you.

www.ingramcontent.com/pod-product-compliance
Lightning Source LLC
Chambersburg PA
CBHW062259290526
45794CB00006B/2614